ISBN 978-0-915545-15-5
First Printing 2013

Published by
Stanley R. Abbott Ministries, Inc.
P.O. Box 533
McRae, Georgia 31055
U.S.A.

On Being Spiritual

PREFACE

> *"For God so loved the world that He gave His only begotten Son, that whoever believes in Him should not perish but have everlasting life."* ***John 3:16***

We understand God giving His only begotten Son meant Jesus would be required to die on the cross as the sacrificial lamb of God to redeem mankind from the power of darkness in order to translate us into the kingdom of God's dear Son. There is no stretch of the imagination in which we can view Jesus' death as the means for our redemption only to leave us to live the exact same lives from which He died to redeem us. That is beyond absurd; it is corrupt! We have been deceived by the subtle craftiness of the enemy. We must awaken to the truth from God and pull down these strongholds of the enemy and everything which exalts itself against the knowledge we have of our God.

The church as a whole on the earth is divided, unskilled, even dysfunctional. How is it possible for any expression of the body of Christ to be so divided, so unskilled, so dysfunctional? Something is terribly, terribly wrong! The answer is so repulsive, so hideous, it is difficult to consider. The current condition of the church on the earth exists as it does because many members of the church have embraced corruptions of the truth as if they are truth.

The purpose of this book is to consider only one truth the enemy has corrupted among us: ***On Being Spiritual***. What does it mean? How have we been deceived? How can we escape the bondage of this deception?

Preface

Table of Contents

Chapter One
THE BEGINNING 1 - 10

Chapter Two
DEVELOPMENTAL BY DESIGN 11 - 16

Chapter Three
CHANGED AT BIRTH 17 - 28

Chapter Four
SPIRIT TO SPIRIT 29 - 40

Chapter Five
SPIRIT TO WORD 41 - 50

Chapter Six
SPIRIT TO HOLY SPIRIT 51 - 68

SUMMARY & CONCLUSION 69 - 74

Table of Contents

Chapter One

THE BEGINNING

Who are we? Who have we become by being born again? It pleased our Father to *"...baptize..."* all of us who believe into Christ as *"...flesh of His flesh and bone of His bone..."* parts of His body! God the Holy Spirit inspired writers of the New Testament to reveal to us...

> *"There is one body and one Spirit, just as you were called in one hope of your calling; one Lord, one faith, one baptism; one God and Father of all, who is above all, and through all, and in you all."* **Ephesians, 4:4-6**

Mysterious and marvelous revelation has been released to us through these same writers regarding who we have become simply by being born again. One of the most remarkable portions of scripture in the entire Bible regarding who we are declares...

> ***"Now to Abraham and his Seed were the promises made. He does not say, "And to seeds," as of many, but as of one, "And to your Seed," who is Christ...****For you are all sons of God through faith in Christ Jesus. For as many of you as were baptized into Christ have put on Christ. There is neither Jew nor Greek, there is neither slave nor free, there is neither male nor female; for you are all one in Christ Jesus.* ***And if you are Christ's, then you are Abraham's seed, and heirs according to the promise."***
>
> *Entire Context is* **Galatians 3:16-29**

As extremely unimaginable, even unbelievable as this Scriptural declaration is, it is nevertheless true.

We are Abraham's seed!

Perhaps it is not any more difficult to believe than any other part of the sovereign plans of God such as: *virgin birth, sacrificial crucifixion, or resurrection of the dead!* It just seems more difficult to imagine or to believe because it is a direct reference to *"...us..."* and to whom *"...we..."* are!

The church on the earth is divided, unskilled, and even dysfunctional. How is it possible for any expression of Christ to be so divided, so unskilled, so dysfunctional? Something is terribly, terribly wrong! The answer is so repulsive, so hideous, it is difficult to consider. The current condition of the church on the earth exists as it does because many members of the church have embraced corruptions of the truth as if they are truth.

We have been deceived by the subtle craftiness of the enemy to believe the corruptions of truth he has sown in our midst! We must awaken to the truth from God and pull down these strongholds of the enemy and everything which exalts itself against the knowledge we have of our God.

The purpose of this book is to consider only one truth the enemy has labored to corrupt among us: ***On Being Spiritual***. What does it mean? How have we been deceived? How can we escape the bondage of this deception?

The Beginning

It is impossible for us to accept that we are...

...flesh and bone body parts of Christ, the resurrected King of all Kings,

...full of the glory of God,

...the righteousness of God in Christ Jesus,

...enabled with divinely empowered faith as a gift from God,

...recipients of the same Spirit who raised Christ Jesus from the dead as an indwelling presence...

...and live like mere men while here on earth, unless it is by choice or deception.

Who would choose to live the lesser if the greater was available? The contrast between whom we have become in Christ through the power of God and how we are living today is not even reasonable to the natural mind.

A television commercial a few years ago advertising some product featured children speaking one at a time emphasizing the absurd:

"When I grow up, I want to be under-paid."

"When I grow up, I never want to be promoted above the glass ceiling."

"When I grow up, I want to be forced into early retirement."

No one would knowingly desire ***less-than***! If a person had ***more-than*** available, I am confident such a person would choose ***more-than***. That is where the deception comes in; the church has simply been ***deceived*** to accept ***less-than.***

This deception begins with how we see. Everything about the new covenant is oriented to spiritual rather than natural. If we do not understand what ***spiritual*** is we will never be able to be ***spiritual*** in practice, even though God has already made us ***spiritual*** in reality. Understanding *"...who..."* God has made us to be, embracing it, and learning how to walk in it are all required in order to make the new covenant work for us. None of these understandings are available to the part of us known as our natural man.

We can easily see the stark contrast between spiritual and natural in Jesus' encounter with Nicodemus. Jesus tells Nicodemus, *"...Most assuredly, I say to you, unless one is born again, he cannot see the kingdom of God..."* Nicodemus did not understand and immediately asked, *"...How can a man be born when he is old? Can he enter a second time into his mother's womb and be born?..."*. Nicodemus was trying to *"...figure out..."* what Jesus meant with his natural mind as a mere man. The Holy Spirit inspired Paul to write to the church at Corinth about this very matter:

> *"Eye has not seen, nor ear heard, nor have entered into the heart of man the things which God has prepared for those who love Him. But God has revealed them to us through His Spirit. For the Spirit searches all things, yes, the deep things of God. For what man knows the*

> *things of a man except the spirit of the man which is in him? Even so no one knows the things of God except the Spirit of God. Now we have received, not the spirit of the world, but the Spirit who is from God, that we might know the things that have been freely given to us by God. These things we also speak, not in words which man's wisdom teaches but which the Holy Spirit teaches, comparing spiritual things with spiritual. But the natural man does not receive the things of the Spirit of God, for they are foolishness to him; nor can he know them, because they are spiritually discerned..."*
>
> ***I Corinthians 2:9-14***

The natural man part of our existence, that is man in his own ability, simply cannot see or receive the things of the Spirit of God. It is important to understand why man in his own ability cannot see the things of the Spirit of God. Paul wrote to the church at Ephesus,

> *"For by grace you have been saved through faith, and that not of yourselves; it is the gift of God, not of works, lest anyone should boast."* ***Ephesians 2:8,9***

Every component of the new covenant requires the ability of God to access it, starting with the *"...authority..."* God grants a person to become a child of God. Man having the ability of God promised as a free gift of the new covenant is a better promise than any promise of the old covenant. The old covenant was based on man doing the will of God in order to obtain the provisions of the covenant in man's own ability. The new covenant is based on man doing the will of God in order to obtain the provisions of the covenant in the ability God *"...gives..."* man. What a marvelous promise! What a marvelous difference!

All of the provisions of the new covenant are designed to produce abundant eternal life for man. If man were able to obtain these provisions in his own ability according to what Paul was inspired to write in his letter to the church at Ephesus, man would be tempted to boast of his own works.

God wants man to understand abundant eternal life cannot be earned; it is a free gift!

Therefore, God has *"...blocked..."* man's natural abilities from being able to *"...see, hear, or understand..."* anything God has prepared for those who love Him.

The church at Corinth demonstrates this shift back to mere-man mindedness after having been born again. Immediately following what is referred to as the second chapter of Paul's letter to the church at Corinth, Paul begins to address the condition of the church.

> *"And I, brethren, could not speak to you as to spiritual people but as to carnal, as to babes in Christ. I fed you with milk and not with solid food; for until now you were not able to receive it, and even now you are still not able; for you are still carnal. For where there are envy, strife, and divisions among you, are you not carnal and behaving like mere men?..."* ***I Corinthians 3:1-3***

Paul's letter was neither accusative nor punitive toward the Corinthians. He was endeavoring to help them see their condition so they could repent and be restored back to spiritual people. Carnal people living and seeing as mere men *"...cannot..."* understand or walk in the provisions of the new covenant. They can only be given ministry which presents opportunity for them to see their condition so they may change.

The church at Corinth demonstrates that new birth itself does not guarantee a person will see spiritually after being born again. Spiritual sight is only available to those who are *"...after the things of the spirit..."* as a way of life. At any time after new birth a person can switch back to desiring the things of the flesh as the priority of his life. Such a shift is defined as being carnally minded. The moment a born again person begins to desire the things of the flesh as the way they live, their sight and ability will shift back to that of mere man.

Our God is laboring with us to help us see what being spiritual means from His perspective. It is merely the condition of a person's heart turned toward the Lord, desiring the things of the kingdom, not some super-Christian spooky thing. I remember a conversation I had with a believer in which the believer sarcastically asked, *"What's the matter, am I not* ***'...spiritual enough...'*** *for you?"* In another encounter another believer said, *"I would do what I know to be the will of God if I were* ***'...more spiritual...'****."* God does not view *"...spiritual..."* in terms of the degree to which a person is spiritual. His perspective of *"...spiritual..."* is always in contrast with *"...carnal..."*, not the degree to which a person is spiritual. God's perspective can be easily seen through the inspired writings of the New Testament.

Look at how God the Holy Spirit inspired Paul to define carnally minded and spiritually minded.

> *"For those who live according to the flesh set their minds on the things of the flesh, but those who live according to the spirit, the things of the spirit. For to be carnally minded is death, but to be spiritually minded is life and peace. Because the carnal mind is enmity against God; for it is not subject to the law of God, nor indeed can be..."* ***Romans 8:5-7***

If we use what Paul was inspired to write defining *"...spiritual..."* from God's perspective and substitute God's perspective into the sayings of the aforementioned believers who had been deceived about being spiritual, they would sound like this, *"What's the matter, do I not* ***'...live according to the spirit enough...'*** *for you?"* or *"I would do what I know to be the will of God if I* ***'...lived according to the spirit more...'****."*

I am confident neither believer understood ***"...being spiritual..."*** equated with ***"...living according to the spirit..."*** or ***"...being after the things of the spirit..."***. I am even more confident that neither believer understood that ***"...not being spiritual..."*** contrasted with ***"...being carnal..."***. God's perspective of spiritual is in contrast with carnal. God makes it absolutely clear *"...spiritually minded..."* is life and peace, *"...carnally minded..."* is death! God our Father's interest in our being *"...spiritual..."* is so we will have life and peace in contrast to death. Any attempt to establish ***"...spiritual..."*** in degrees rather than just accepting that spiritual is in contrast to carnal is argumentative. Such argumentativeness will hinder or stop altogether God's will from becoming a reality in a person's life.

If degrees of spiritual were acceptable in God, the church at Corinth could have rebutted Paul's letter with, *"What's the matter, are we not spiritual enough for you?"* or *"We would do what we know to be the will of God if we were more spiritual."* The folly is so clear here. We have already stated Paul was not accusing nor punishing the church at Corinth; he was trying to help the church be restored. It is the will of God for all who believe to live as spiritual people! That is, living according to the spirit because they are after the things of the spirit.

We have been able to be deceived because we have not been spiritual people. We have tried to *"...figure out..."* what God desires for us just like Nicodemus did. The only way to escape from the bondage of our deception is to accept that we will never understand God's will in our own ability. We must embrace that God's design for the church is oriented to the spiritual rather than the natural. Three things are required in order to make the new covenant work for us:

1. ***We must understand who God has made us to be.***
2. ***We must embrace our new identity.***
3. ***We must learn how to walk as spiritual people.***

We must accept that none of these understandings are available to the part of us known as our natural man.

We must accept that God has designed us to be spiritual people!

Chapter Two

DEVELOPMENTAL BY DESIGN

Just as the Creator carefully designed and crafted the universe so, too, He carefully designed and crafted the church. Most things regarding the church are developmental by design. That is, *"...process..."* is a fundamental part of our development. For example: Mankind's entrance into the church, or new believer's growth in the church, even salvation itself is designed to be walked out in fear and trembling on a daily basis. Life in the spirit is parallel to life in the natural world. Both are developed in stages and phases requiring ***patience***, ***process***, and a ***strategic plan*** to ensure progress.

Perhaps we could obtain understanding as to why God crafted the church to be developmental by design, but, at this stage, it is most important just to know that He did. We apply this understanding by rejoicing for whatever *"...mystery..."* He reveals to us by eating it as food from our God required to nourish and sustain us until our hunger for more causes another heavenly meal to be released.

Scripture declares, *"...whoever calls on the name of the Lord shall be saved."* Consider the *process* involved in giving *"...whomsoever..."* the opportunity to call on the name of the Lord. Anyone can call on the Lord in order to be saved, but how will they be able to call on Him in whom they have not believed? ...or believe in Him of whom they have not heard?

Webster's New Universal Unabridged Dictionary defines *"...process..."* as continuing development involving many changes, or a particular method of doing something, generally involving a number of steps or operations. Process for *"...whomsoever..."* to be able to call on the Lord involves someone being sent to preach to the one who has not heard that Jesus has become Lord. They then preach to give opportunity for the hearer to believe in Jesus and ultimately to call on Him to be their Lord.

> *"...How then shall they call on Him in whom they have not believed? And how shall they believe in Him of whom they have not heard? And how shall they hear without a preacher? And how shall they preach unless they are sent?..."* ***Romans 10:14,15***

In order for a person to be sent to *"...preach..."* to another concerning Jesus, the person being sent must have first heard of Christ and received Him to be Lord for himself.

This type of *"...process..."* began with Jesus Himself. When He walked on the earth with His disciples, He revealed what He had already freely received from His Father as the way they were to live. His life was a living testimony of what He had received from the Father as the way He and His disciples were to live on earth. Jesus' life and the way He lived with His disciples was the seed from which the life of the church was ordained to grow. In the same process we have already seen in ***Romans 10:14,15***, this life and the way it was designed to be lived is to be passed on. The process begins with a person who knows the truth providing opportunity for another person who does not know the truth to know it.

If we do not understand the church *"...is developed in stages and phases requiring* ***patience, process****, and a* ***strategic plan*** *to ensure progress..."*, then the enemy, with all subtleness, will have opportunity to embed a corruption of the truth into our midst. One of the primary components of his corruption involves ***process***. A natural world illustration will help show *"...how..."* ***process*** works.

This natural world illustration involves children and the skill of shoe tying. Jimmy knows how to tie shoes, Billy does not. Jimmy offers to teach Billy how to tie shoes, and Billy accepts. With relative ease Billy learns how to tie shoes. No special lesson plans were necessary, no special fasting or praying was required, no agony over the prospects of having to *"...teach..."* Billy. No one imposed this responsibility on Jimmy to have to help his friend, Billy. It was simply a child having a skill who saw his friend without the skill and offered to help him.

There are two persons involved in the ***process*** in this natural world illustration: the one who knows how to tie shoes and the one who does not. The one who knows how to tie shoes needs to be confident he actually knows how and must be willing to help his friend learn. The one who does not know how to tie shoelaces must desire to learn and be willing to receive help from his friend.

The enemy has been able to embed his corruption into the church because we have not understood the purpose or the sheer simplicity of God's design. God's purpose is so the unskilled may become skilled as the means to walk according to His design. This *process* involves actual training and time for one person to help another person develop the skills he desires!

In the natural world illustration no one directed the child with skills to help his friend. The relationship between the two children motivated the child with skills to help his friend. We are to freely give revelation of Christ to the lost so they may be saved and to unskilled believers to help them learn how to walk according to God's design. Our relationship with Christ and with the person in need will serve to motivate us to freely give what we have so freely received.

God's ***strategic plan*** required for life in the spirit to be developed is also full of simplicity. The old covenant needed to be replaced because it was based on man's ability to do the will of God. The new covenant was established on better promises than the old covenant. The better promises revolve around man being able to do the will of God in the ability of God. However, this great promise has a ***glitch!*** Man cannot wield the power of God as a mere man. The only way man can handle the power of God as the means of doing the will of God is to be born again and to live as a spiritual person.

We have already seen the results of Nicodemus trying to *"...figure out..."* what being *"...born again..."* meant with his natural mind. Nicodemus demonstrated how limited man was under the old covenant using only the power of natural man. Natural man cannot see or do the things of God successfully in his own ability.

Because this simple understanding from God has been so corrupted by the subtle craftiness of the enemy, another scriptural illustration may help to show the difference between the abilities of natural man versus spiritual man. Perhaps the most tender and poignant illustration in the entire New Testament is Mary Magdalene seeing the Risen Lord.

> *"Mary stood outside by the tomb weeping, and as she wept she stooped down and looked into the tomb. And she saw two angels in white sitting, one at the head and the other at the feet, where the body of Jesus had lain. Then they said to her, "Woman, why are you weeping?" She said to them, "Because they have taken away my Lord, and I do not know where they have laid Him." Now when she had said this, she turned around and saw Jesus standing there, and did not know that it was Jesus. Jesus said to her, "Woman, why are you weeping? Whom are you seeking?" She, supposing Him to be the gardener, said to Him, "Sir, if You have carried Him away, tell me where You have laid Him, and I will take Him away." Jesus said to her, "Mary!" She turned and said to Him, "Rabboni!" (which is to say, Teacher). Jesus said to her, "Do not cling to Me, for I have not yet ascended to My Father; but go to My brethren and say to them, 'I am ascending to My Father and your Father, and to My God and your God.'"* **John 20:11-17**

At first Mary saw the Lord with her natural eye, the same eye with which she would have looked to see the gardener. However, scripture is clear the natural part of man cannot receive the things from the Spirit of God. No matter how hard she looked at the man standing before her with her natural eye, she could not have seen who He really was. Then, when Jesus spoke to her again, calling her name to reveal who He really was, she turned her ***heart*** toward the Lord. The veil of her natural ability which had covered her spiritual eyes was removed, and she saw the Risen Christ.

Just as Mary could not see Jesus with her natural eye, neither can we. We will only see a *"...gardener..."* if we look naturally, no matter how hard we try. Only when we see ourselves as spiritual will Christ be revealed in our circumstances.

Seeing, possessing, and living in the provisions of the new covenant is only possible by accepting and using the power God has given to new creatures. The old covenant did not produce the results God desired because man could not see or do the will of God in his own ability. The new covenant will only work if man accepts God's power as the only way to do God's will. Here is a truth of profound importance:

God is the one who made us spiritual;
it is up to us to "...learn..." to walk as spiritual people.

Accepting the truth that we are spiritual is a singular act of faith. That is, we do not learn to accept the truth that we are spiritual through process, we simply accept it by faith when this truth is given to us. However, learning to walk as a spiritual person is developmental by design.

Chapter Three

CHANGED AT BIRTH

Jesus' conversation with Nicodemus regarding new birth is pregnant with meaning from Heaven. The very instant a person is born again radical life changes occur.

> *"...Therefore, if anyone is in Christ,* ***he is a new creation*** *(2937);* ***old things have passed away, behold, all things have become new...*** *"* ***II Corinthians 5:17***

> ***2937 ktisis*** from *2936* ; original *formation* (prop. the act; by impl. the thing, lit. or fig.): -- building, creation, creature, ordinance.

> ***2936 ktizo*** prob. akin to *2932* (through the idea of the *proprietorship* of the *manufacturer*); to *fabricate*, i.e. *found* (*form* originally): -- create, Creator, make.

Several parts of this verse provide us with so much hidden information the words almost explode when you read or say them. We know from Scripture that anyone who is born again has been baptized into Christ and is referred to from new birth onward as being *"...in Christ..."*. Is this merely an intellectual connection with Christ?

Mankind is made spirit, soul, and body in the image of God. Therefore, if being *"...in Christ..."* is not merely an intellectual connection, then we have to be *"...in Him..."* with one, two, or all of our three parts.

This cannot be a reference to our natural physical selves. We are not all naturally, physically in Christ. This leaves either our soul or spirit parts to be in Christ. Which of the two is it? ...or both? Turning again to Jesus' conversation with Nicodemus, immediately following Nicodemus' question about how a man can be born when he is old, Jesus provides us with the answer we seek.

> *"...Most assuredly, I say to you, unless one is born of water and the Spirit, he cannot enter the kingdom of God. That which is born of the flesh is flesh, and that which is born of the Spirit is spirit. Do not marvel that I said to you, 'You must be born again.'..."* ***John 3:5-7***

Here Jesus speaks plainly that being born again is not referring to the natural man. Being born again is a reference to the spirit man. The moment man is born again His spirit is made a brand new creation. ***The significance of this change to the spirit of man cannot be over-emphasized!***

The new life man acquires as a result of accepting Jesus as Lord is oriented to his spirit, not his natural physical body or his soul. Certainly, the introduction of the life of God into a man's spirit is going to have influence on the other two parts of man, his soul and his body. However, the life the newly born again man experiences and must learn to live is with his spirit in the spiritual realm.

If through subtle craftiness the enemy can corrupt man's understanding of new birth so that man does not *"...see..."* being born again is oriented to the spiritual realm, then the enemy can contain the effects of new birth to the natural realm. If the enemy is successful in his efforts, being born again will lose its intended purpose for man while man is still living on planet earth. In effect, man will continue to live as he always has prior to new birth in the abilities he has as a mere man. The intent of our God is for man to be born again, enter the new covenant, and live in the abilities given to him by God.

New birth, baptism into Christ, and becoming a new creation were all immediate results of a person's acceptance of Jesus as Lord. However, learning to live as a new creation in Christ is developmental by design. A person enters Christ as a babe-in-Christ and is expected to desire the pure milk of the word that he may grow thereby. This growth will continue through little child, young man, and adult stages. All growth is a direct result of growing in the knowledge of God. This knowledge is only available to the spirit of man in the spiritual realm. If man succumbs to the devastating effects of the corruption sown by the enemy, then growth will not occur in his life while he still lives on earth. He will be a born again, in-Christ, new creation but remain a babe-in-Christ as long as he remains natural realm oriented. The changes which occurred in his life at new birth will have lost their value to give him a new way to live while remaining here on earth.

The next explosive part of ***II Corinthians 5:17*** is the instant we were born again *"...old things passed away..."*. Without a spiritual orientation these words are just words, without any real meaning and will not change the way we live.

In Paul's letter to the church at Rome he was inspired by God the Holy Spirit to address this very issue.

> *"...For as by one man's disobedience many were made sinners, so also by one Man's obedience many will be made righteous. Moreover the law entered that the offense might abound. But where sin abounded, grace abounded much more, so that as sin reigned in death, even so grace might reign through righteousness to eternal life through Jesus Christ our Lord. What shall we say then? Shall we continue in sin that grace may abound? Certainly not! How shall we who died to sin live any longer in it? Or do you not know that as many of us as were baptized into Christ Jesus were baptized into His death? Therefore we were buried with Him through baptism into death, that just as Christ was raised from the dead by the glory of the Father, even so we also should walk in newness of life. For if we have been united together in the likeness of His death, certainly we also shall be in the likeness of His resurrection, knowing this, that our old man was crucified with Him, that the body of sin might be done away with, that we should no longer be slaves of sin. For he who has died has been freed from sin..."* ***Romans 5:19-6:7***

The part of our existence which was baptized into Christ's death was not our natural physical body. However, the Father accepts our faith's identification with Christ's death as if we did actually die with Him. In this way, *"...old things passed away..."* from us through death. Unless we can see this *"...truth..."* in the spirit we will reason it away with our natural mind.

In the same letter to the church at Rome Paul told them,

> *"...Reckon yourselves to be dead indeed to sin, but alive to God in Christ Jesus our Lord. Therefore do not let sin reign in your mortal body, that you should obey it in its lusts. And do not present your members as instruments of unrighteousness to sin, but present yourselves to God as being alive from the dead, and your members as instruments of righteousness to God. For sin shall not have dominion over you, for you are not under law but under grace. What then? Shall we sin because we are not under law but under grace? Certainly not! Do you not know that to whom you present yourselves slaves to obey, you are that one's slaves whom you obey, whether of sin leading to death, or of obedience leading to righteousness?..."* **Romans 6:11-16**

Every single aspect of the revelation contained within the context of this portion of Scripture has been under assault by the enemy ever since it was written. The enemy is terrified that we might begin to see with our spirit what God has freely given to us in Christ. The moment we begin to see the truth with our spiritual eyes that old things have passed away and we are new creations capable of deciding whether we sin or not, we will begin to break the stronghold of the enemy in our lives. All traditional sayings established by the doctrine of men will lose any real meaning. We will see them as merely excuses. Sayings such as...

> *"All men sin, it is impossible not to sin until we get to heaven."*

> *"Oh, I know we sin, but God knows our heart."*

> *"I know we sin, but we are only human."*

All of these sayings and a myriad more just like them are a direct result of men seeing the provisions of the new covenant in the abilities they have as mere men. Only if we see ourselves as God has made us to be, spiritual people, and begin to learn the way of the spirit in the spiritual realm will we ever fulfill our destinies in God.

Here is a pivotal understanding we must obtain if we are going to live and move and have our being in Christ successfully. Paul, writing by inspiration of God the Holy Spirit, wrote to the church at Galatia *(...to us, too...)...*

> *"...Now to Abraham and his Seed were the promises made. He does not say, "And to seeds," as of many, but as of one "And to your Seed," who is Christ..."*
>
> ***Galatians 3:16***

The new covenant promises of God were only made to Abraham and his Seed who is Christ. It pleased God the Father to place all of the provisions of the new covenant ***in Christ***. New covenant promises were not made to all of us, only to Abraham and to his Seed who is Christ.

If believers are going to partake of these promises, we can only do so by ***living*** in Christ. We have already seen it is our spirit which is in Christ. That means living as spiritual people is required in order to successfully live and move and have our being in Christ. This includes partaking of the promises of the new covenant. This changes everything!

Consider this abbreviated list of the promises Scripture specifically lists as ***only*** available in Christ:

salvation	***II Timothy 1:9 & 2:10***
promise of life	***II Timothy 1:1***
redemption	***Romans 3:24***
new creation status	***II Corinthians 5:17***
one body	***Romans 12:5 & Galatians 3:28***
righteousness	***I Corinthians 1:30***
sanctification	***I Corinthians 1:30***
redemption	***I Corinthians 1:30***

While Paul was waiting for Silas and Timothy in Athens on one occasion, he approached Mars Hill, also known as the Areopagus. Here he found religious men who regularly gathered to consider new things. He garnered their attention and began to speak to them:

> *"Men of Athens, I perceive that in all things you are very religious; for as I was passing through and considering the objects of your worship, I even found an altar with this inscription: To The Unknown God. Therefore, the One whom you worship without knowing, Him I proclaim to you..."* ***Acts 17:22,23*** *(Context verses 16-31)*

In this time of ministry Paul, speaking of Jesus, said...

> *"...for in Him (Jesus) we live and move and have our being..."* ***Acts 17:28***

Jesus often taught people using natural world illustrations knowing they would compare what they understood about the natural world with what He was teaching about the spirit world. Because it pleased our God to make us flesh and bone parts of Christ's body, our lives must be lived in Him all the time. The only living place any of our natural body parts can remain alive is connected to the natural body. If a natural body part is cut off, it immediately begins to die. The only way to keep it alive is to keep it connected to the natural body. In a parallel fashion the only living place any of the spiritual body parts can remain alive is connected to Christ.

"...In Him we live and move and have our being...!"

Dad asked you to go to the tool shed to pick up a tool for him while he is working on the lawn mower in the back yard. The family dog likes to hang around the tool shed. The dog is huge, and you are little. You want to be a part of your Dad's project, but the very thought of that huge dog sends shivers up and down your spine. Your Dad sees your reservation and says, "I'll go with you; there is something else I need you cannot reach" *(even though he is just going to help allay your fears)*. He takes you by the hand and off you go, hand in hand with your Dad. Sure enough that 'ol dog comes running right at you when your Dad says, "Whoa," and the dog stops. Your fear goes away, and you feel like you could do anything or go anywhere if you were hand in hand with your Dad.

Mom just baked your favorite cookies; they are still steaming hot on the cookie rack, smelling all wonderful. You were not old enough to go to school yet; you were at home with Mom all the time. Mom had to leave the kitchen to go use the rest room. She left you with strict instructions not to touch the cookies. You were so little, the cookies were your favorites, and the smell was drivin' you crazy. Just one, you reasoned. Mom was gone a little longer than expected. When she returned, you had chocolate chips dripping from your lips and more than one cookie devoured. A small child will typically act differently outside of Mom's presence than in her presence.

Simple illustrations involving little children, but, oh, how they serve us. It is the will of God that you and I live and move and have our being in Christ. The external presence of Dad and Mom in the previous illustrations changed the child's perspective. More intimate than just being in His external presence, we have actually been made a living part of Christ. We are one with Him as His flesh and bone body.

Being one with Christ will give us a sense of boldness and confidence to do anything He asks because we know He is united right there with us as we do His will. It will also help us choose righteously when confronted with a temptation to stray. All of these things can only be done in faith by spiritual people. And they are to begin at the time of our new birth. God makes us spiritual people by His design the moment we are born again. It is up to us to learn to walk as spiritual people through the process of our growth in the knowledge of Him.

Consider the difference between actually being *"...one..."* with Christ, always united with Him, versus being a believer with a traditional mindset regarding your relationship with Christ. Matthew recorded Jesus as saying,

> *"All authority has been given to Me in heaven and on earth. Go therefore and make disciples of all the nations, baptizing them in the name of the Father and of the Son and of the Holy Spirit, teaching them to observe all things that I have commanded you; and lo, I am with you always, even to the end of the age."*
>
> ***Matthew 28:18-20***

Traditionally, the church has viewed this mandate of the Lord this way: Christ who has become Lord and has received all authority in heaven and on earth is *"...sending..."* us to the nations. He will release the necessary authority for us to be able to do whatever He *"...sends..."* us to do. ***Webster's New Universal Unabridged Dictionary*** defines "...*send...*" as, "...to appoint to go with authority to represent; as, to *send* an ambassador to a foreign court; to *send* an agent to negotiate business."

Compare a New Testament use of the English term *"...sent..."* translated from the Greek text in a similar context.

> *"Whoever calls on the name of the Lord shall be saved. How then shall they call on Him in whom they have not believed? And how shall they believe in Him of whom they have not heard? And how shall they hear without a preacher? And how shall they preach unless they are* ***sent (649)****?"* ***Romans 10:13-15***
>
> ***sent 649 apostello*** from *575* and *4724*; *set apart*, i.e. (by. impl.) to *send out* (prop. on a mission) lit. or fig.: -- put in, send (away, forth, out), set [at liberty].

If the church uses the dictionary, either English or Greek, to determine the meaning of *"...send..."* regarding our being sent by Christ, we will not see correctly. Lexicographers may define terms for us, but they must not define our relationship with Christ in any matter. Instead, our relationship must be defined by the revelation we receive from our God; we are Christ's flesh and bone body parts. Our relationship with Christ is not as part of a giant clearing house with people constantly coming and going as Christ directs them here and there. Truly, He does send us here and there, but not where He remains in one place, and we go to another.

The writer of the letter to the Hebrew Christians at the conclusion of his letter quoted an Old Testament scripture from Deuteronomy the thirty-first chapter. The context was Moses speaking to Israel and to Joshua regarding Joshua's new role as leader set to lead Israel across the Jordan into the Promised Land. The quote in the letter to the Hebrew Christians says,

> *"For He Himself (God) has said, "I will never leave you nor forsake you." So we may boldly say: "The Lord is my helper; I will not fear. What can man do to me?"*
>
> ***Hebrews 13:6***

Just another understanding we have from our God to help us change our traditional mind-set. When Christ sends us on a mission, He is not dispatching us out away from Him to go somewhere while He stays behind. When Christ sends us on a mission, He goes together with us because we are parts of the exact same body and because He has promised never to leave us nor to forsake us.

Traditionally, when Christ sends us somewhere, our perspective has been that He dispenses a corresponding measure of authority to us so we may fulfill our assignment in the authority He has given us. Alternatively, as Christ and I go together as parts of the same body, wherever He chooses for us to go, we go together with Him in His body where all of the authority in heaven and on earth has been placed. Now, we can go where He sends us and do what He asks of us with the understanding that we go one with Christ, as parts of the same body, abiding where He and all of His authority resides, knowing He is right there with us helping us fulfill our task.

The traditional perspective is not altogether lacking. After all, tradition sees it is Christ who is sending us, and He is the One giving us the authority to do His will. However, God's perspective is that Christ goes united with us where ever He chooses for us to go because we are parts of the same body together, both of us living where all authority in heaven and on earth resides, and ***together*** we fulfill His will!

Our baptism into Christ took place by the design and power of God the moment we were born again. Becoming a flesh and bone part of the body of Christ was a change made in our lives by God at the time of our new birth. There is nothing anyone can do to earn this place in Christ; it is a free gift from our God. However, we do have a part in learning to live in Christ. The same God who gave us our place in Christ as a free gift assigned us the task of growing in the knowledge of Him. In a parallel fashion to a new-born natural infant being required to learn the natural skills necessary to live in this natural world, so, too, a new-born in Christ is required to learn the spiritual skills necessary to live in Christ in the spirit world.

Chapter Four

SPIRIT TO SPIRIT

Jesus often taught in parables. One of his parables, the parable of the sower, is of such importance Matthew, Mark, and Luke all three recorded it. After Jesus spoke this parable to the people, His disciples came to Him and asked why He had spoken in parables. Jesus' answer is very remarkable for His disciples both then and now.

> *"Because it has been given to you to know the mysteries of the kingdom of heaven, but to them it has not been given. For whoever has, to him more will be given, but whoever does not have, even what he has will be taken away from him. Therefore I speak to them in parables, because seeing they do not see, and hearing they do not hear, nor do they understand. And in them the prophecy of Isaiah is fulfilled, which says:*
>
>> *'Hearing you will hear and shall not understand, and seeing you will see and not perceive; for the hearts of this people have grown dull. Their ears are hard of hearing, and their eyes they have closed, lest they should see with their eyes and hear with their ears, lest they should understand with their hearts and turn, so that I should heal them.'*
>
> *But blessed are your eyes for they see, and your ears for they hear; for assuredly, I say to you that many prophets and righteous men desired to see what you see, and did not see it, and to hear what you hear, and did not hear it."* ***Matthew 13:11-17***

"It has been given to you to know the mysteries of the kingdom of heaven...!" Truly a remarkable thing Jesus said to His disciples, but He is talking to us today as much as He was to them then. It is the will of God for Jesus' disciples to know and understand the mysteries of the kingdom of heaven. We are a special and chosen people.

> *"You are a chosen generation, a royal priesthood, a holy nation, His own special people, that you may proclaim the praises of Him who called you out of darkness into His marvelous light; who once were not a people but are now the people of God, who had not obtained mercy but now have obtained mercy."* ***I Peter 2:9,10***

Did God arbitrarily or randomly select us? Did He look down from heaven and select us like a shopper selects one piece of fruit over another at the market? How did we become His special and chosen people?

Going back to Jesus' encounter with Nicodemus we find the first part of this mystery revealed which serves as the beginning to the answer we seek. Jesus told Nicodemus...

> *"...For God so loved the world that He gave His only begotten Son, that whoever believes in Him should not perish but have everlasting life. For God did not send His Son into the world to condemn the world, but that the world through Him might be saved..."* ***John 3:16,17***

God did not arbitrarily or randomly select us like a shopper selects one piece of fruit over another at the market. God loves the whole world and desires for all men to be saved.

"Therefore I exhort first of all that supplications, prayers, intercessions, and giving of thanks be made for all men, for kings and all who are in authority, that we may lead a quiet and peaceable life in all godliness and reverence. For this is good and acceptable in the sight of ***God our Savior, who desires all men to be saved and to come to the knowledge of the truth****."*

I Timothy 2:1-4

"The Lord is not slack concerning His promise, as some count slackness, but is longsuffering toward us, ***not willing that any should perish but that all should come to repentance****."* ***II Peter 3:9***

"All authority has been given to Me in heaven and on earth. Go therefore and make disciples of all the nations, baptizing them in the name of the Father and of the Son and of the Holy Spirit, teaching them to observe all things that I have commanded you; and lo, I am with you always, even to the end of the age."

Matthew 28:18-20

It is easy to see from Scripture that God loves all men everywhere and that He does not desire for any men anywhere to perish. So, then, how did you and I become His own special and chosen people out of all the men of the world if it was not arbitrary and random selection?

Our selection was based on our *"...response..."* to the knowledge of Him who has been given to us. Not everyone responds in faith from the heart.

"He came to His own, and His own did not receive Him. But as many as received Him, to them He gave the right to become children of God, to those who believe in His name; who were born, not of blood, nor of the will of the flesh, nor of the will of man, but of God." ***John 1:11-13***

Paul wrote in His letter to the church at Rome that...

> *"...whoever calls on the name of the Lord shall be saved. How then shall they call on Him in whom they have not believed? And how shall they believe in Him of whom they have not heard? And how shall they hear without a preacher? And how shall they preach unless they are sent?"* ***Romans 10:13-15***

Out of God's love and desire for all men to be saved, He is sending the church into all the world to tell all nations who Jesus is so that all may have opportunity to be saved. Anyone who hears who Jesus is can call on the Lord, and they will be saved. However, we know that not all men who hear who Jesus is will respond in faith to that knowledge. Jesus went to His own but His own did not receive Him, so, too, many today hear of Jesus as Lord but refuse to receive Him. Those who receive Him will be saved to become God's own special and chosen people, the sons of God!

The difference between those who receive Jesus and those who do not is the heart. A person whose heart is closed to change and unwilling to do the will of God will not know what God wills. During Jesus' earthly ministry His knowledge of God was wonderful to some but baffling to others. At the time of the Feast of Tabernacles there was division among the people regarding Jesus. Some thought Jesus was good, and others thought He was a deceiver. Scripture says Jesus taught in the temple during the feast and the Jews *"...marveled, saying, "How does this Man know letters, having never studied?"* Jesus' answer to them is relevant to our consideration regarding man's ability to know the will of God.

"My doctrine is not Mine, but His who sent Me. If anyone wills to do His will, he shall know concerning the doctrine, whether it is from God or whether I speak on My own authority." ***John 7:16,17***

Here is one of the *"...keys of the kingdom..."!*

A person must be willing to do the will of God before he can know what God wills.

How is this possible? How can we be willing to do what God wills even before we know what He wills? The answer is of profound importance to our lives.

The priority of our submission is to our God, not to His will!

We bow down in love and faith to Him in response to His first love for us. We trust Him! We have confidence that whatever He wills for us is going to produce abundant eternal life for and through us.

The prophet Jeremiah prophesied to man living under the old covenant of this very subject. James wrote in his epistle regarding who God is and how He relates to man under the new covenant.

"For I know the thoughts that I think toward you, says the Lord, thoughts of peace and not of evil, to give you a future and a hope." ***Jeremiah 29:11***

> *"Let no one say when he is tempted, "I am tempted by God"; for God cannot be tempted by evil, nor does He Himself tempt anyone... Every good gift and every perfect gift is from above, and comes down from the Father of lights, with whom there is no variation or shadow of turning. Of His own will He brought us forth by the word of truth, that we might be a kind of firstfruits of His creatures."* Entire Context ***James 1:12-18***

Jesus demonstrated a willingness to do the will of God unlike any other man before Him. Even at the point of His impending death on the cross Jesus was willing to do the will of His Father. Over and over again Jesus repeatedly spoke this truth in one form or another:

> *"For I have come down from heaven, not to do My own will, but the will of Him who sent Me."* ***John 6:38***

> *"Father, if it is Your will, take this cup away from Me; nevertheless not My will, but Yours, be done."*
> ***Luke 22:42***

But why was Jesus so willing to do the will of God? Was it merely raw submission done in faith to what He knew to be God's will? Was Jesus' priority submission to the will of God? Perhaps we can begin to construct an answer using the parable of the prodigal son ***(Luke 15:11-32)*** illustrating a son's submission to his father's will as his priority. Most know the story from the perspective of the younger of two sons who asked for his inheritance, left his father, spent all on riotous living, came to his senses, and returned home just to be a servant in his father's house realizing how foolish he had been. However, the older of the two sons provides us with an understanding about how having a priority to do your father's will can be misguided.

The older of the two sons became angry when he saw how his father had received his younger brother back into the family. He was so stricken with his condition he would not even go in to join the celebration. So, his father came out and pleaded with him. The eldest son's reply and subsequent exchange with his father is going to change our whole understanding about doing the will of God.

> *"Lo, these many years I have been serving you; I never transgressed your commandment at any time; and yet you never gave me a young goat, that I might make merry with my friends. But as soon as this son of yours came, who has devoured your livelihood with harlots, you killed the fatted calf for him."* ***Luke 15:29,30***

There is no scriptural refutation of the eldest son's statement declaring his obedience and faithfulness to serve his father. It appears his declaration was true. He did serve his father faithfully and never transgressed any of his father's commandments. However, his statement demonstrates a heart full of bitterness, resentment, and even hatred toward his brother and his own father. He believed he was *"...entitled..."* to provisions for making merry with his friends. He believed his entitlement was based on having served and obeyed his father for many years.

His father's reply will reveal a horrible corruption operating in the son from the enemy. His father said...

> *"Son, you are always with me, and all that I have is yours. It was right that we should make merry and be glad, for your brother was dead and is alive again, and was lost and is found."* ***Luke 15:31-32***

The very first word of the father's reply is so powerful: *"Son"*. From this son's father's perspective his priority was on his relationship with his son, not on his son's obedience and faithfulness to have obeyed and served. The father's next words reveal the eldest son's lack of understanding about his relationship with his father. The father said, *"...you are always with me, and all that I have is yours..."*. Consider the meaning of these words. The father was telling his eldest son he could have had anything for which he had asked. We know this represents the character of this son's father toward his sons because he had already given his youngest son his inheritance when he had asked.

This eldest son had devoted himself to doing his father's will, desiring to be rewarded, but never had his desires fulfilled. What a miserable life! The father desired for his sons to have abundance and was incredulous at the fact that all he owned was available to both sons, but the eldest never availed himself of any of it. How is that possible? The eldest son had abundance available to him simply by being his father's son but never partook of any of it. Further, he was bitter, resentful, and angry because he did not have what he desired. The simple truth is the eldest son placed his priority on doing his father's will instead of having a loving relationship with his father. ***What corruption!***

Most certainly Jesus did His Father's will! However, Jesus did His Father's will out of love and sonship toward His Father, not out of diligent, faithful obedience. Here is an important understanding:

- ***A person can do the Father's will without any love or sonship involved.***

- ***A person who loves Abba, seeing the proper role-relation of sonship as priority, will do the Father's will because of love and sonship.***

A person living life without any love or sonship involved as described in the first example above will live like the eldest son in the parable of the prodigal son. A person living life described in the second example above will live like Jesus. ***The choice is clear!***

We have been chosen to know the mysteries of the kingdom of heaven because we turned our heart toward the Lord and received Jesus as Lord. Growth in the knowledge of these mysteries causes us to see Him as He is. This sight, in turn, enhances our relationship of love and sonship motivating us to do His will.

Everything about the kingdom in relation to us revolves around our ability to *"...see, hear, and understand..."* what is being revealed to us. Jesus spoke in parables to a people who... *"...seeing they do not see, and hearing they do not hear, nor do they understand.."*. What is the difference between us and them? How did Jesus know the Father to be able to love Him? How did Jesus understand His role as son? If we cannot find answers to these questions, we will never be able to be the person who loves Abba, seeing the proper role-relation of sonship as priority, or be motivated to do the Father's will.

Anything that has to do with the new covenant can only be known through the ability God provides us to know it. The old covenant operated in the ability of man. The new covenant operates in the ability God gives man! Therefore, whenever any person *"...sees, hears, or understands..."* the things of the kingdom, it is exclusively because that person has received the ability God has given him to be able to do so. Conversely, whenever any person cannot *"...see, hear, or understand..."* the things of the kingdom, it is exclusively because that person has not received the ability of God to be able to do so.

We have already stated, *"...the difference between those who receive Jesus and those who do not is the* ***heart****. A person whose heart is closed to change and unwilling to do the will of God will not know what God wills..."*. A person whose heart is open to change and willing to do the will of God will know what God wills because God *"...imparts..."* His ability into such a person so that person may be able to *"...see, hear, and understand..."*. This principle of the kingdom is really, really simple:

A willing heart open to change and to do the will of God will partake of the ability of God!

Everything about the new covenant is heart to heart, that is ***"...spirit to spirit..."!*** It is a man's spirit that becomes a new creation at the time of his new birth. It is a man's spirit that is baptized into Christ. It is a man's spirit that connects with God the Holy Spirit. Everything about man's relationship with God is designed by God to be ***"...spirit to spirit..."***. Any time man attempts to alter God's design in any way, especially reverting back to his own abilities operating through his natural man parts, that man will short-circuit the abilities given to him by God. The new covenant will not work for a person living as a mere man. The new covenant will only work for a person living as a spiritual man.

Jesus knew the Father and was able to love Him because Jesus lived as a spiritual man. Jesus understood His role as son because He lived as a spiritual man, connected as ***"...one..."*** with His Father. The moment you and I understand how God designed the new covenant to operate and embrace our lives as spiritual men, only then will we begin to flourish in the new covenant, ***spirit to spirit!***

Chapter Five

SPIRIT TO WORD

Just after Jesus spoke the parable of the sower ***(Matthew 13:1-23; Mark 4:1-20; & Luke 8:4-15)*** to the masses He explained the parable to His disciples. His explanation provides three important revelations regarding the ministry of the word.

> *"...Therefore hear the parable of the sower: When anyone hears the word of the kingdom, and does not understand it, then the wicked one comes and snatches away what was sown in his heart..."* ***Matthew 13:18,19***

The first revelation to consider is ***"...the word is sown directly into the heart of the hearer..."***. Because it is God who designed the new covenant, He provides for those who receive His word to be able to *"...see, hear, and understand..."* what they are receiving. God desires for all men to be saved. He goes to extraordinary lengths to give man opportunities to be saved and to grow in the knowledge of Him.

Whenever a believer speaks the word in faith to another person, God causes that word to be supernaturally planted directly into the *"...heart..."* of the hearer. If the hearer is willing to change and do the will of God, God gives the hearer the ability to understand what has been planted in him. Seed planted into the heart of the hearer and divinely empowered ability to understand it are God's provisions for men to know Him. They are ***gifts*** from a loving benevolent God and cannot be earned.

The second revelation to consider is ***"...it is a lack of understanding on the part of the hearer which causes the seed sown in his heart to be snatched away...".*** This lack of understanding is the result of a very specific action taken by the hearer. At the time of planting the hearer will decide whether he is open to change and willing to do what the seed just planted has shown him to be the will of God. If the person decides he is not open to change and will not do the will of God, his choice will block the supernatural ability from God and keep it from working on his behalf.

It is extremely important to understand that God does not withhold His ability from such a person. The person's choice stops God's ability from working on his behalf. God will not impose His ability on anyone. The only ability such a person will have under these conditions is his own ability as a natural man to understand God's word. Such a person will *"...see but not see, and hear but not hear, nor will he understand..."* what he has received as seed sown in his heart.

The third revelation to consider is ***"...the wicked one is the thief who steals the word planted as seed from the heart of the hearer...".*** The hearer's unwillingness to change by not doing the will of God is what gives the enemy opportunity to steal the seed which had been sown in his heart. The wicked one does not have direct access to man's spirit, but he can see the hearer's non-response to the word of God. He immediately employees the same subtle device he used to deceive Eve in the Garden of Eden: He plants thoughts challenging the truth of the word of God.

A person willing to change and do the will of God receives divinely empowered abilities to understand the seed sown in his heart. This divinely empowered ability also serves to block the thieving activity of the wicked one and to protect the newly planted seed. A person unwilling to change and do the will of God stops the ability God desires for him to have and opens the door for the enemy to continue ruling in his life. The enemy will take full advantage of any opportunity given to him.

The three revelations provided by Jesus' explanation of the parable of the sower have been specifically applied to one person planting the word as seed into another person and the immediate results of that planting. One thing needs to be pointed out here. Any person at any time may take the seed another person planted in his heart into his private study at a different location and time from which the seed was planted for further meditation without the seed being stolen.

The considerations already made on the three revelations regarding the ministry of the word were not intended to be exclusive in the way a person partakes of the word nor how the Holy Spirit may teach a person the meaning of the word. They were intended to reveal to what lengths our God will go to help a person know Him. Further, these considerations were intended to reveal how much better the new covenant is than the old covenant. The better promises of the new covenant were made by our God because of His love for us and His desire to see us actually be able to live in the covenant He has made with us. He knows any covenant He makes with us will have to be based on the abilities He provides in order for us to keep covenant with Him.

Once the seed of the word has been received in faith and understanding wrought through the ministry of the Holy Spirit that word becomes a living and active part of our ***spirit***. This notion is imperative to our understanding in order for the word as a living and active part of our spirit to produce the will of the Father for us. The new covenant will *"...explode..."* in activity and productivity when the church sees and embraces the simple truth that the word of God will only produce life out of the abundance of our ***spirit!***

Consider the words of Jesus as recorded by John:

> *"I am the bread of life. He who comes to Me shall never hunger, and he who believes in Me shall never thirst."*
>
> ***John 6:35***

Jesus used the natural world illustrations of hunger and thirst to give us a glimpse into the type of connection He desires for us to have with Him. Peter used this same comparative type of illustration when writing to those who had just been born again.

> *"...as newborn babes, desire the pure milk of the word, that you may grow thereby, if indeed you have tasted that the Lord is gracious..."* ***I Peter 2:2,3***

Whether *bread* or *milk* the concept is the same, eating food as the sustenance required to live.

The natural body is mysteriously and wondrously made. It has the ability to break down the foods we eat, to extract their nutrients, and to be nourished by them. There is a saying in the natural world; *"You are what you eat."* Surely this is just an extreme or overly simplified way of expressing the wonder of the body's ability to break down the foods we eat and make them part of the body.

This concept can be taken to extremes. A certain company created a T.V. commercial using this concept to promote their product. The commercial showed a person eating a donut. As they walked away the donut became a part of their hips. Funny, disgusting perhaps, but, oh, how we know it to be true. We are what we eat, even to extremes!

We do not have to fully understand the science of nutrition to *"...get..."* the meaning of this natural world illustration. Jesus and Peter's use of natural world illustrations involving food to compare believers' connection with the Lord were designed by God the Holy Spirit to give us an easy way to see how we are to live in the kingdom. We are to view receiving the knowledge of Him as partaking of *"...food..."*. We are to understand that all revelation from our God is to be *"...partaken..."* of as food or drink for our spirit. The knowledge we are given from Him is designed to be life to us. Our spirits have been designed to receive input from the Holy Spirit so the *"...nutrients..."* from the spiritual food we eat and drink become *"...life..."* to us. This life is to be the means for us to live in the power of our God.

This mysterious and wondrous process takes place in our spirit. It is not an intellectual exercise like learning vocabulary words for your natural mind. It is an *eating-digesting-living* process for our spirit to be done in faith. Any time a believer refuses to accept this *eating-digesting-living* process as God's design, or explains the design away with mere-man reasoning, he will short-circuit the process keeping his spirit from benefiting from spiritual food. Any time a believer receives the ministry of the word with his natural mind short-circuiting occurs when the food is partaken.

Another similar condition is possible which will stop the process from working. This condition occurs in a different manner but produces the same result: *The spiritual food stops producing the life our God intends.* This condition can best be explained using a natural world illustration involving a child's toy. Etch-a-sketch is a toy on which a child can draw by turning two knobs on the front lower corners of the toy. The toy can then be turned upside down and shaken to erase what was drawn. If a believer partakes of spiritual food in faith as a spiritual person causing the food to become a living active part of his spirit but then reverts back to mere-man mindedness, the spiritual food stops producing life. This works almost exactly like etch-a-sketch: The word was written in the believer's spirit, but when he turned back to mere man, what was present and working is removed or at least stopped from producing. Several churches written about in the New Testament demonstrate this condition.

The church at Corinth had previously received knowledge regarding offices of ministry as gifts from God. Every aspect of the letters Paul was inspired to write to the church emphasized a focus on Christ not man. The church knew the offices of ministry were called by God for the purpose of bringing them the knowledge of Christ. Paul stated it over and over again in many ways throughout the course of his letters to them. However, instead of the church receiving that knowledge and allowing it to glorify Christ, they exalted the ministers who had brought them the knowledge. Any believer who sees only as a mere man can be deceived into believing God intended for the church to exalt the ministers given by Christ! Paul specifically stated this error operating within the church at Corinth was a direct result of their seeing as mere men as opposed to seeing as spiritual people.

The church at Laodicea is perhaps the ultimate illustration of believers' reverting back to mere man mindedness stopping the life of God from working in their lives. Jesus Himself brought correction, even rebuke, to this church regarding their condition. He told them,

> *"...Because you say, 'I am rich, have become wealthy, and have need of nothing' -- and do not know that you are wretched, miserable, poor, blind, and naked -- I counsel you to buy from Me gold refined in the fire, that you may be rich; and white garments, that you may be clothed, that the shame of your nakedness may not be revealed; and anoint your eyes with eye salve, that you may see. As many as I love, I rebuke and chasten. Therefore be zealous and repent. Behold, I stand at the door and knock. If anyone hears My voice and opens the door, I will come in to him and dine with him, and he with Me..." Entire Context* ***Revelation 3:14-22***

This church was so mere man minded they believed they actually needed nothing. Their blindness had even caused them to shut Jesus out of their lives as a way of life. It was as if they were saying, *"We've got this"!* Oh, how foolish, how blind, how carnal. Their reverting back to mere man mindedness short-circuited the productivity of their spiritual sight. Jesus called them ***"...blind..."!*** What had once been written in their spirit was no longer visible to them.

The church made up primarily of Jewish believers demonstrates this condition, too. The writer of this letter told the church...

> *"...For though by this time you ought to be teachers, you need someone to teach you again the first principles of the oracles of God; and you have come to need milk and not solid food..."* ***Hebrews5:12***

These believers had received the basic principles of the doctrine of Christ and had grown significantly enough so they *"...ought to be teachers..."*. However, the ministry gift responsible for stewarding the word and monitoring their lives found them to have gone backward. Like the etch-a-sketch, what had once been written in their hearts needed to be written all over again.

The word of God can manifest in many forms. In Jesus' explanation of the parable of the sower He explained the process of the word being ministered from person to person involved the word of God being planted into our heart *(our spirit)* as seed. Can you imagine the word of God in *"...seed..."* form?

As Solomon prayed at the dedication of the temple which he built in Jerusalem, he expressed his inability to imagine how the Creator of the whole universe would be able to dwell inside of the temple he had just built ***(II Chronicles 6:12-18)***. Solomon even tried to *"...negotiate..."* with God for Him to just keep His eyes and ears turned toward the temple ***(II Chronicles 6:19-40)*** instead of actually dwelling in it. It is not our job to negotiate with our God regarding His will. It is our job just to accept God's will God's way. It was Jesus Himself who said when the word of God is ministered; it is planted as a seed into the heart of the hearer. This is the manifestation of the word He has chosen for the new covenant.

This seed is not just any seed; it is the word of God! Because God is a spirit no matter how God manifests Himself, all manifestations will have *"...spirit..."* as their foundational component. The seed of the word spoken by a believer planted into another person is spiritual as opposed to mental, intellectual, or physical. When this seed is planted in the spirit of man, the place of God's choosing, it immediately becomes active, ready to produce God's desired result. The disciples who encountered Jesus on the road to Emmaus said to one another,

> *"Did not our heart burn within us while He talked with us on the road, and while He opened the Scriptures to us?"* ***Luke 24:32***

Everything about the new covenant is designed to be spiritual. The born again new creature's spirit is designed to be able to receive the seed of the word of God and to immediately experience the power of the word. The spirit of man is designed to receive the seed of the word and ministry from the Holy Spirit. The Holy Spirit will reveal Christ according to the knowledge contained within the seed so we may have the same kind of life Christ has. Jesus said,

> *"And this is eternal life, that they may know You, the only true God, and Jesus Christ whom You have sent."*
> ***John 17:3***

Our spirit is designed to partake of the life which is in the seed and make it the very life we live. This is the will of God: The life of the seed of the word is to become our own life! In order to make this a reality we absolutely have to understand how our spirit has been designed to function in relation to the word of God.

Our spirit and the word of God are to be partners!

Chapter Six

SPIRIT TO HOLY SPIRIT

"Eye has not seen, nor ear heard, nor have entered into the heart of man the things which God has prepared for those who love Him. But God has revealed them to us through His Spirit. For the Spirit searches all things, yes, the deep things of God. For what man knows the things of a man except the spirit of the man which is in him? Even so no one knows the things of God except the Spirit of God. Now we have received, not the spirit of the world, but the Spirit who is from God, that we might know the things that have been freely given to us by God. These things we also speak, not in words which man's wisdom teaches but which the Holy Spirit teaches, comparing spiritual things with spiritual. But the natural man does not receive the things of the Spirit of God, for they are foolishness to him; nor can he know them, because they are spiritually discerned. But he who is spiritual judges all things, yet he himself is rightly judged by no one. For who has known the mind of the Lord that he may instruct Him? But we have the mind of Christ..."
I Corinthians 2:9-15

Immediately following this portion of Scripture, Paul used what he had just written to address a mind-set which needed adjusting in the church at Corinth. He wrote,

"...And I, brethren, could not speak to you as to spiritual people but as to carnal, as to babes in Christ. I fed you with milk and not with solid food; for until now you were not able to receive it, and even now you are still not able; for you are still carnal. For where there are envy, strife, and divisions among you, are you not carnal and behaving like mere men?" ***I Corinthians 3:1-3***

The contrast being made here is between the spirit part of believers as opposed to their mere man parts. The natural part of a believer being considered here, his natural mental or intellectual mind cannot receive things from the Spirit of God. God designed the new covenant to work in the spirit, spirit to spirit. Believers are designed to receive things from the Holy Spirit with their spirit: ***spirit to Holy Spirit!***

We have already stated in chapter four, *"Any time man attempts to alter God's design in any way, especially reverting back to his own abilities operating through his natural-man parts, that man will short-circuit the abilities given to him by God. The new covenant will not work for a person living as a mere man. The new covenant will only work for a person living as a spiritual man."* God's design for the new covenant to function through our spirit is better than any way of any covenant He has previously made with mankind. Why would we try to negotiate with our God for Him to allow us to connect with the Holy Spirit with any part of our natural selves?

His way is best! Our way is not!

The way of God for all participants of the new covenant is the way of the spirit. The lives mankind lives before partaking of the new covenant are lived oriented to the natural world. These natural world lives begin as newborn infants, no exceptions. No matter what social, economic, racial, or national base into which the newborn is birthed, everyone has to learn the way of the natural world into which such a one has been birthed.

Consider one of these learning experiences in which everyone must grow: *learning to walk.* When a newborn grows sufficiently to be able to learn to walk, acquiring this new skill is a process. No one stands up and begins to walk successfully from his first step. Everyone must *"...learn..."* to walk. That is, this skill begins with just a single step, then another, and another, until the child is walking successfully. Unfortunately, there are typically a lot of *"...falls..."* involved in the process. Some of the falls may even be violent. Nevertheless, the child somehow continues to desire to learn to walk.

Some scientific study most likely exists regarding the psychology of a child's desire to learn to walk. However, without delving into the science of the matter, surely we could all agree children do continue the learning process until they achieve success in learning to walk. Adults know walking is better than crawling as a means of going from one place to another. Perhaps the child continues the process simply because he is motivated by an adult who has the perspective of walking versus crawling in which the adult understands how much better walking is than crawling.

Maybe a child's desire would not be sufficient on his own to motivate himself to continue the process without the involvement of an adult. The easiest conclusion we can make regarding the type of motivation required in the learning-to-walk process comes from the understanding that walking is so much better than crawling. A child's ultimate motivation to learn to walk will typically, then, come from a person who has this perspective.

Because the new covenant is spirit based, everyone who enters the new covenant must *"...learn..."* to walk in the spirit, no exceptions. The enemy has used one of his subtle devices to deceive many in the church into believing that because the new covenant is founded on the abilities God gives us, rather than our own abilities, we will operate successfully in those abilities because they are gifts from God without having to *"...learn..."* to operate in them.

More than 35 years of ministry have given me a wealth of experiences with members of the body of Christ. One of the most remarkable deceptions I ever encountered came from a believer who said, *"My Father loves me too much to let me make a mistake."* This statement is void of understanding that life in the kingdom is developmental by design. While life in the kingdom is certainly not *"...trial-n-error..."* based, it does require growth in knowledge, understanding, and skills to be walked out successfully. The New Testament accounts of believers growing in Christ paints a completely different picture from their *"...Father loving them too much to let them make a mistake...."*.

The Holy Spirit's relationship and ministry to believers had a wonderful beginning. Just prior to Jesus' crucifixion and subsequent departure from the earthly connection He had with His most intimate disciples He promised them another *"...Helper..."* to be involved with them after His departure.

> *"If you love Me, keep My commandments, and I will pray the Father, and* ***He will give you another Helper****, that He may abide with you forever -- the Spirit of truth, whom the world cannot receive, because it neither sees Him nor knows Him; but you know Him, for* ***He dwells with you and will be in you****..."* ***John 14:15-18***

In the next three chapters of ***John*** Jesus identifies the roles of the Holy Spirit in relation to believers.

> *"...the Helper, the Holy Spirit, whom the Father will send in My name,* ***He will teach you all things****, and* ***bring to your remembrance all things that I said to you****..."*
> ***John 14:26***

> *"...when the Helper comes, whom I shall send to you from the Father, the Spirit of truth who proceeds from the Father,* ***He will testify of Me****..."* ***John15:26***

> *"...I still have many things to say to you, but you cannot bear them now. However, when He, the Spirit of truth, has come,* ***He will guide you into all truth****; for He will not speak on His own authority, but whatever He hears He will speak; and* ***He will tell you things to come****.* ***He will glorify Me****, for He will take of what is Mine and declare it to you. All things that the Father has are Mine. Therefore I said that He will take of Mine and declare it to you."* ***John 16:12-15***

The ministries *(roles)* of the Holy Spirit to believers are:

...Helper...

...Teacher...

...Reminder...

...Guide...

...Foreteller...

...Glorifier...

The point of connection believers have with the Holy Spirit in order to be able to receive ministry from Him is our spirit. The spiritual lives of every born again believer begins as newborn infants, no exceptions. No matter who the person is, what social, economic, racial, or national base they have in the natural world, everyone begins as a newborn infant and has to learn the way of the spirit world into which they have been birthed.

Just like in the natural world, everyone in the spiritual world has to *learn to walk.* Slight differences exist between the two learning experiences, but fundamentally they are parallel. A newborn in the spirit world begins immediately to learn to walk in the spirit. It is his successful walking skills which take him forward in God. Motivation for the newborn to begin this process and continue it to completion will come from gifts of ministry given by Christ and fellow believers who understand that all life in the new covenant requires learning to walk successfully in the spirit.

Any time any believer reverts back to walking like a mere man, it is the Lord's will for someone who is *"...spiritual..."* to help restore such a one back to his spiritual walk if that is possible. The new covenant will not work for a mere man minded person. It will only work for the spiritually minded, for those who have learned or are learning how to walk in the spirit. This is God's design and must not, cannot be altered by man!

Spirit To Holy Spirit

This spirit to Holy Spirit connection represents a form of communication. Effective communication is only possible by properly identifying roles. In order for our communication to be effective with the Holy Spirit we begin by accepting the *"...roles..." (ministries)* we have already seen He has been given by the Father on our behalf. The Holy Spirit is as eager to do the will of the Father as was Jesus during His earthly ministry. Our part of the process is to learn how this spiritual communication works and to grow in our communication skills.

Jesus said, *"...My sheep (191) hear My voice (5456)..."*. Jesus has a voice He wills for His sheep to hear.

> ***191 akouo*** a prim. verb; to *hear* (in various senses): give (in the) audience (of), come (to the ears of), ([shall]) hear (-er,-ken), be noised, be reported, understand.
>
> ***5456 phone*** prob. akin to *5316* through the idea of *disclosure*; a *tone* (articulate, bestial or artificial); by impl. an *address* (for any purpose), *saying* or *language*: -- noise, sound, voice.
>
> ***Strong's Exhaustive Concordance of the Bible***

Believers frequently say today, *"I heard the Lord say ...thus and such..., and what He said was almost audible."* The meaning here is completely contradictory. Whatever a person *"...hears..."* must be *"...audible..."* in order to be *"...heard..."*. If a thing was not audible, it could not be heard; it would be inaudible. ***Webster's New Universal Unabridged Dictionary*** defines *inaudible* as not able to be heard.

The Lord has a voice, and it is His will for His sheep to *"...hear..."* His voice. His voice must be audible in order for it to be heard. His voice is a spiritual voice and is audible to the spiritual ear in the spiritual world *(unless He makes it audible to the natural ear which is His prerogative)*. His voice is most definitely audible; it is just not audible in the natural world. When a person makes the completely contradictory statement they *"...heard the Lord and it was almost audible...",* surely what they mean is it was almost audible to their natural ear. The new covenant has been designed to operate in the spirit world rather than the natural world. This design includes hearing!

Too often believers want to alter God's design, many times out of fear. Jesus did not say He would give His sheep impressions or feelings or a sense. He said His sheep would hear His voice. Although, Jesus can give us impressions or feelings or a sense about a thing He desires for us to know. We cannot discount these forms of communication. However, we must not discount His spiritually audible voice which can be heard.

Because Jesus told us plainly, *"...My sheep hear My voice..."*, there must be a way for us to safely do this without fear of interference or interruption from the wicked one. Jesus' design for His church is not so tenuous, so dangerous, that only the really brave or really mature can participate. I honestly do not know how the church, the body of Christ, ever thought that Jesus would design a form of communication for His body which would easily put us in harm's way. Surely this is just another device from the enemy to keep us from learning to ***"...hear..."!***

The Lord provides divinely empowered protection for us. When we turn our heart toward the Lord in faith, this action activates a divinely empowered shield around us. In Paul's second letter to the church at Corinth he gave us a glimpse into these matters.

> *"...clearly you are an epistle of Christ, ministered by us, written not with ink but by the Spirit of the living God...Not that we are sufficient of ourselves to think of anything as being from ourselves, but our sufficiency is from God, who also made us sufficient as ministers of the new covenant, not of the letter but of the Spirit; for the letter kills, but the Spirit gives life...Therefore, since we have such hope, we use great boldness of speech -- unlike Moses, who put a veil over his face so that the children of Israel could not look steadily at the end of what was passing away. But their minds were blinded. For until this day the same veil remains unlifted in the reading of the Old Testament, because the veil is taken away in Christ. But even to this day, when Moses is read, a veil lies on their heart. Nevertheless when one turns to the Lord, the veil is taken away. Now the Lord is the Spirit; and where the Spirit of the Lord is, there is liberty. But we all, with unveiled face, beholding as in a mirror the glory of the Lord, are being transformed into the same image from glory to glory, just as by the Spirit of the Lord." Entire Context* ***II Corinthians 3:1-18***

The glory of the Lord serves to protect us so that what we behold is exclusively from the Lord. Anytime our heart is turned toward the Lord this protective shield is active on our behalf.

In another place in Scripture Luke records Jesus' words speaking about the same subject, using a different illustration:

> *"So I say to you, ask, and it will be given to you; seek, and you will find; knock, and it will be opened to you. For everyone who asks receives, and he who seeks finds, and to him who knocks it will be opened. If a son asks for bread from any father among you, will he give him a stone? Or if he asks for a fish, will he give him a serpent instead of a fish? Or if he asks for an egg, will he offer him a scorpion? If you then being evil, know how to give good gifts to your children, how much more will your heavenly Father give the Holy Spirit to those who ask Him!"* **Luke 11:9-13**

What Luke recorded Jesus as saying makes it absolutely clear our heavenly Father is responsible to protect us as we seek Him and the things of His kingdom. We can trust our Father and our God!

If you are hearing the voice of the Lord, then you are doing so in faith because your heart is turned toward Him. This action, heart turned toward the Lord in faith, keeps our protective shield activated. Go ahead; listen to what the Lord desires to say to you without fear! He has made a way for us to safely hear His voice. Just remember you must listen with your spiritual ear while your heart is turned to the Lord. If you try to alter this design and hear with your natural ear, your actions will lower your shield and you will place yourself at risk.

The spirit to Holy Spirit connection we have is in the spiritual world. The Holy Spirit does not communicate with our natural mind or intellect because we have already seen in Scripture that our natural man parts do not receive things from the Holy Spirit. It is necessary to say it is the Holy Spirit's prerogative to speak to us so our natural man parts can *"...see, hear, or understand..."*, but this is the exception.

For example, when John the Baptist baptized Jesus in the River Jordan, there was a manifestation of God available to the natural parts of the men who observed this baptism. Men could hear God the Father's voice with their natural ears and see the Holy Spirit as a dove with their natural eyes. ***(Matthew 3:13-17; Mark 1:9-11; Luke 3:21,22; John 1:29-34).*** The ***"...rule..."*** of our connection is spirit to Holy Spirit in the spirit world. Only God can make exceptions...

The ministries *(roles)* of the Holy Spirit to: *"...help us, ...teach us, ...remind us what Christ has said to us, ...guide us, ...foretell to us things to come, ...glorify Christ to us"*, will all be fulfilled as we ***receive*** such ministry from Him. Scripture has already shown us we receive ministry from the Holy Spirit with our spirit. Now, how do we do that? Maybe, a better question is how does the Holy Spirit provide ministry to us?

The believers' encounter with the Holy Spirit on the Day of Pentecost points us in the right direction.

> *"When the Day of Pentecost had fully come, they were all with one accord in one place. And suddenly there came a sound from heaven, as of a rushing mighty wind, and it filled the whole house where they were sitting. Then there appeared to them divided tongues, as of fire, and one sat upon each of them. And they were all filled with the Holy Spirit and began to speak with other tongues, as the Spirit gave them utterance (669)."*
>
> ***Acts 2:1-4***

669 apophtheggomai from *557* and *5330*; to *enunciate* plainly, i.e. *declare*: -- say, speak forth, utterance.

Strong's Exhaustive Concordance of the Bible

utterance

1. the act of uttering, or expressing by voice.
2. the power or style of speaking.
3. that which is uttered; especially, a word or words, whether written or spoken.
4. the act of uttering, or circulating.

Webster's New Universal Unabridged Dictionary

Scripture says, *"...they were all filled with the Holy Spirit and began to speak with other tongues, as the Spirit gave them utterance..."*. Extracting accurate meaning from this Scripture is essential to promote understanding regarding how the Holy Spirit provides ministry to believers. The term *"...they..."* refers to the believers. The believers were all filled with the Holy Spirit and *(the believers)* began to speak with other tongues. *"As the Spirit gave them utterance..."* refers to the Holy Spirit giving them utterance.

If the believers were able to speak with other tongues on the basis of the utterance given to them by the Holy Spirit, then it is accurate to acknowledge the believers had to have received the utterance given by the Holy Spirit. Giving utterance is the same thing as speaking. Receiving utterance is the same thing as hearing. This *speaking and hearing model* of communication took place between the Holy Spirit and the believers in the spirit: ***Holy Spirit to spirit***.

It is fully acceptable to use a natural world illustration to help explain something in the spirit world. However, care must be taken not to take a natural world illustration beyond the point of acceptable meaning. For example, believers are referred to as the sheep of Jesus' pasture. Taking this illustration beyond the point of acceptable comparative meaning would be to expect us to begin growing wool or bleating.

Communication between the Holy Spirit and believers in the context of speaking with other tongues is just such a natural world illustration we must not take beyond the point of acceptable meaning. The *speaking and hearing model* in the natural world cannot be used exactly the same to compare communication between the Holy Spirit and believers in speaking with other tongues. The Holy Spirit giving utterance ***"...is..."*** the Holy Spirit speaking. Receiving utterance from the Holy Spirit ***"...is..."*** believers hearing what the Holy Spirit is speaking. However, this *speaking and hearing model* *"...functions..."* differently in the spirit than it does in the natural world.

In the spirit, there are several spiritual components present which are not present in the natural world model. Firstly, the Holy Spirit is inside of the believer speaking directly to the believer's spirit. Secondly, the believer hears with a divinely empowered faith used in this case to be able to hear with the ability God is providing with which to hear. Thirdly, there are no interrupting forces between man's new creation spirit and the Holy Spirit. This communication is protected from interference by God Himself.

Consider another internal form of communication, which is not a *speaking and hearing model*, but is communication nonetheless. This form of communication takes place inside of humans in the natural world. If a person touches the hot surface of a stove with his fingertip, data is sent to the brain identifying the condition. Upon receiving the message the brain processes it and sends a reply saying, *"...remove fingertip from the hot surface..."*. While scientists can explain this communication in their own medical and scientific terms, it is sufficient for our purposes to identify it as a form of communication wherein *"...a message is sent from the fingertip to the brain and back again..."*. This communique takes only a fraction of a second from beginning to end. The person does not have to wait an appreciable amount of time while experiencing pain waiting for the data to be sent, processed, and returned. Everything happens in measures of time difficult for us to understand.

The *speaking and hearing model* used between the Holy Spirit and believers in the process of giving and receiving utterance is more like the fingertip illustration than two humans carrying on a conversation in the natural world. Perhaps a better illustration would be the simultaneous translation provided by a good language interpreter. Within this translation process everything is happening so fast it is difficult to identify when the actual translation occurs. When a believer speaks in other tongues using utterance he has received from the Holy Spirit, the communication between the Holy Spirit and the believer is a simultaneous action. Nevertheless, it is a *speaking and hearing model*, just not of the natural world.

One other question must be asked and answered in our quest for developing our communication skills with the Holy Spirit. With what does the Holy Spirit ***speak*** utterance to the believer? The concept of *"...being spoken to..."* can be used in an extended sense. A person may say, *"That artist's painting really spoke to me."* The person making such an assertion does not mean the painting actually *"...spoke..."* to him. Instead, the person means the painting conveyed some type of message to him, typically an emotional response provoked by the subject matter of the painting. This does not fit into the *speaking and hearing* communication model of which we are concerned. Unlike the inanimate painting, the Holy Spirit really does speak to us. The *speaking and hearing* communication model of which we are concerned is the actual speaking done by one party and the actual hearing of another party. Using these parameters we can assert that speaking in this sense is done with the voice, and hearing is done with the ears.

Because the Holy Spirit actually speaks to the believer to *"...give utterance..."*, then it is accurate to say the Holy Spirit has a voice. Jesus told us, *"My sheep hear My voice."* ***(John 10:27)***. The Father spoke from heaven saying, *"This is My beloved Son, in whom I am well pleased!"* ***(Matthew 3:17)***. The Father and the Son as two parts of the Godhead both have voices. It is not difficult to accept that the Holy Spirit also has a voice, especially in the light of our discoveries regarding the concept of His giving utterance. We can say, then, any time a believer speaks in other tongues provided by the Holy Spirit, that believer is hearing the voice of the Holy Spirit.

We have determined the location for communication between the Holy Spirit and the believer is in the spirit. Is there a more precise location available? For example, each of us lives in a certain geographic location. We can begin identifying that location in general terms, reducing the location to more specific terms like concentric circles within a larger circle. I live in the United States of America, in the State of Georgia, in the county of...etc., etc., etc., until I pinpoint my residence and my exact location within my residence *(currently, upstairs in my office, sitting in front of my computer)*.

The communication between believers and the Holy Spirit takes place in the spirit world, inside of us *(Jesus said the Holy Spirit, "...will be in you..." **John 14:17**)*, but where within us? It is of great significance to determine this location. Jesus provides guidance in this matter as we read Jesus' words speaking about the promise of the Holy Spirit recorded by John.

> *"On the last day, that great day of the feast, Jesus stood and cried out, saying, "If anyone thirsts, let him come to Me and drink. He who believes in Me, as the Scripture has said, out of his heart (2836 [belly - **KJV**]) will flow rivers of living water." But this He spoke concerning the Spirit, whom those believing in Him would receive; for the Holy Spirit was not yet given, because Jesus was not yet glorified" **John 7:37-39***
>
> ***2836 koilia*** from koilos (*"hollow"*); a *cavity*, i.e. (spec.) the *abdomen*; by impl. the *matrix*; fig. the *heart*: -- belly, womb.
>
> ***Strong's Exhaustive Concordance of the Bible***

Any way you interpret Jesus' words recorded by John in ***John 7:38***, figuratively or literally, He has just given us the location from which the water of the Holy Spirit flows within the believer. The ***New King James*** version of the Bible has chosen to use the term *"...heart..."* as the English translation for the Greek term *"...koilia..."*. The ***King James*** version has chosen to use the term *"...belly..."*. ***Strong's*** defines the Greek term *"...koilia..."* as *"...belly, womb...",* and only in a figurative sense as *"...heart.."*. In an effort not to create our understanding from some nuanced meaning of a Greek term defined by a concordance, whether heart, belly, or womb, it is clear the actual location from which the water of the Holy Spirit flows is somewhere within the lower torso of man.

Determining this location is of particular significance to help us avoid the possible corruption from the enemy that the Holy Spirit speaks to our natural mind or intellect. Our natural mind or intellect does not operate out of our lower torso but, rather, out of our head. The Holy Spirit does not speak to our mind or intellect but to our spirit. The location for this communication to our spirit is somewhere within our lower torso.

Speaking with other tongues is the simplest and safest way to develop your communication skills with the Holy Spirit. It can only be done in faith as the ability provided by God. The Holy Spirit is the One giving the utterance, and God Himself guards the process from interference. Speak with other tongues with confidence rehearsing what you know about the process:

1. ***The Holy Spirit is giving you the utterance.***
2. ***He gives you utterance by speaking to you.***
3. ***You are receiving utterance from Him.***
4. ***You receive utterance from Him by hearing His voice.***
5. ***This communication originates in your lower torso.***
6. ***What you receive flows up and out of your mouth.***
7. ***God is guarding this process.***

The more familiar you become with this spiritual process, the more you will become skilled at recognizing the Holy Spirit's input and the channel within you through which tongues flow. The voice the Holy Spirit uses to give you the utterance for you to speak is the exact same voice He uses to fulfill all of His other roles to you. Soon you will recognize His voice and respond to it with ease, and your spirit to Holy Spirit communication skills will be developing wonderfully!!!

SUMMARY & CONCLUSION

Everyone who has been born again has been baptized into Christ as a part of His *"...flesh and bone..."* body! We have become the *"...Seed of Abraham..."*, and *"...heirs according to the promise..."*. Many in the church on the earth have been living under a blanket of deception believing they are just mere men, living in their own abilities, doing the best they can, waiting for their transition to heaven.

Everything in the new covenant is oriented to spiritual as opposed to natural. This spiritual orientation is God's design. He designed the covenant to have this spiritual orientation so we could wield His power as spirit beings. Any time anyone refuses to see themselves as God has recreated them to be, a spiritual person, such a person will not be able to live successfully on the earth in Christ.

Our lives in the new covenant must undergo developmental change. All of us began our journey as newborn babes in Christ. We are designed to grow through the stages of little child, young man, all the way to adult in the spirit. This growth is a process.

The new covenant was established on better promises than the old covenant. The basis for all of the better promises is that every participant of the new covenant will have the abilities of God as their source of life rather than their own abilities as mere men.

The moment a person is born again *"...he becomes a new creation; old things pass away...all things become new..."*. This radical change at the time of new birth occurs to man's spirit, not his body or soul. A refusal to accept this change and begin seeing ourselves as spiritual people will give the enemy continued power in our lives. Our way of life will remain unchanged just as if we had not been born again. The abilities of God will not work in our lives as mere men. We will have bound ourselves to an old covenant way of life, based on doing the will of God in our own abilities as mere men.

If we see ourselves as God has made us to be, spiritual people, we will view everything differently. We will see our baptism into Christ as having given us right of access to all He has and all He is. We will cast off old sayings and our old way of life based on tradition and the doctrine of men. We have been captives to tradition and the doctrine of men long enough. ***It is time to go free!***

We are God's own special and chosen people. It is the will of God that you and I *"...know the mysteries of the kingdom of heaven..."!* It is the will of God that all men might be saved becoming His own special and chosen people. However, we know all will not receive Jesus as Lord. Such a person's refusal to accept Christ stops them from becoming one of God's own special and chosen people. They *"...will hear and not understand, see and not perceive..."* the word of God which is planted in their heart. Our acceptance of Jesus brought us into special and chosen relationships with our God making us able to know the mysteries of the kingdom of heaven.

Our submission must be to our God rather than to His will. Jesus taught we must be willing to do His will in order to know His will. The only way we will be willing to do God's will before we know what He wills is to have love, confidence, and trust in our God. This love, confidence, and trust in our God come as a result of having received His love for us first. The priority of our submission must change from submitting to do God's will to submitting to our God! The difference is beyond compare...

The eldest son in the *Parable of the Prodigal Son* demonstrates submission and service to do his father's will but with corrupt priorities. This eldest son was full of bitterness, resentment, even hatred. His priorities were based on faithfulness and service to do his father's will, not love and sonship for his father. We must extricate ourselves from this hideous trap of submission based on faithfulness and service and begin to be faithful and serve out of our love and sonship for our Father.

We are designed to be faithful and to serve only as Jesus did. Jesus was faithful and served out of His love for His Father and His sonship to His Father. We must be faithful and serve the same way as Jesus did, not like the eldest son from the *Parable of the Prodigal Son.* We will live life like the eldest son in the parable if we see ourselves as mere men. We will only be able to live life like Jesus if we see ourselves as spiritual men. Seeing ourselves accurately will open the door for us to live ***spirit to spirit*** in the new covenant with our God and with one another.

Spiritual orientation applies to the ministry of the word, too. Jesus told us *"...when anyone hears the word of the kingdom...it is planted like a seed into his heart (spirit)..."*. If the hearer is willing to change by doing the will of God, he will be given divinely empowered abilities to understand the word he hears when it is planted as a seed within his heart. If he refuses to change and will not do the will of God, he will not be able to understand the word he hears. His lack of understanding, based on his unwillingness to change and do the will of God, gives the enemy right to steal the seed which is planted in his heart.

The word of God is designed to be necessary food for the sons of God by which to live and grow. Believers partaking of the word as food from heaven and seeing themselves as spiritual people cause what they have eaten to begin to be digested within them. Soon that process of digestion will produce new life within them. Believers have been designed to live in the power of this new life as a way of life.

Living life as a *"...spiritual person..."* is God's design for the new covenant. This provision of the covenant is *"...better..."* than any provision from any previous covenant. We must stop trying to negotiate with our God to get Him to allow us to live as natural men.

His way is best! Our way is not!

Just as natural world infants must learn to walk in the natural world, so, too, spiritual world infants must learn to walk in the spirit. This includes learning how to see and to receive ministry from the Holy Spirit. He has been given to be our *"...Helper, Teacher, Reminder, Guide, Foreteller, and Glorifier of Christ..."*. However, none of these roles operate automatically simply because they are God's will. We must activate them just like we activate Jesus' role as Lord and Savior in order to be saved. This process can only be done in relation to the Holy Spirit: ***spirit to Holy Spirit***.

The Holy Spirit has a voice as does the Father and Jesus. We must learn to hear His voice in order to receive from Him. God has given us an easy way for this to happen. The Holy Spirit will abide within us, speaking to our spirit from within us. We will be able to hear His voice with a divinely empowered faith giving us the ability to do so. God Himself protects this entire process from outside interferences. It is safe to learn how to hear the voice of the Holy Spirit if we do it God's way as a spiritual people.

Our God has carefully designed and crafted every part of the new covenant! We have been brought into covenant relationship with Him fully able to be a functional part of the covenant in the abilities God Himself has given us . The only condition we must meet is that we live in the covenant with Him His way, not our own! We have divinely empowered abilities to do this...

Nothing can hold us back except our own will!!!

www.ingramcontent.com/pod-product-compliance
Lightning Source LLC
Chambersburg PA
CBHW071837020426
42331CB00007B/1764

* 9 7 8 0 9 1 5 5 4 5 1 5 5 *